WHO EATS WHAT?

OCEAN FOOD CHAINS

by Rebecca Pettiford

pogo

Ideas for Parents and Teachers

Pogo Books let children practice reading informational text while introducing them to nonfiction features such as headings, labels, sidebars, maps, and diagrams, as well as a table of contents, glossary, and index.

Carefully leveled text with a strong photo match offers early fluent readers the support they need to succeed.

Before Reading

- "Walk" through the book and point out the various nonfiction features. Ask the student what purpose each feature serves.
- Look at the glossary together. Read and discuss the words.

Read the Book

- Have the child read the book independently.
- Invite him or her to list questions that arise from reading.

After Reading

- Discuss the child's questions. Talk about how he or she might find answers to those questions.
- Prompt the child to think more. Ask: What other ocean animals and plants do you know about? What food chains do you think they are a part of?

Pogo Books are published by Jump!
5357 Penn Avenue South
Minneapolis, MN 55419
www.jumplibrary.com

Copyright © 2016 Jump!
International copyright reserved in all countries. No part of this book may be reproduced in any form without written permission from the publisher.

Library of Congress Cataloging-in-Publication Data

Pettiford, Rebecca, author.
  Ocean food chains / by Rebecca Pettiford.
    pages cm. – (Who eats what?)
  Audience: Ages 7-10
  Includes index.
  ISBN 978-1-62031-302-2 (hardcover: alk. paper) –
  ISBN 978-1-62496-354-4 (ebook)
  1. Marine ecology–Juvenile literature. 2. Food chains (Ecology)–Juvenile literature. 3. Marine animals–Juvenile literature. I. Title.
  QH541.5.S3P48 2016
  577.7–dc23
                                              2015025216

Series Editor: Jenny Fretland VanVoorst
Series Designer: Anna Peterson
Photo Researcher: Anna Peterson

Photo Credits: All photos by Shutterstock except: Alamy, 10-11; Corbis, 3; Dreamstime, 1; Getty, cover, 14, 18-19; Nature Picture Library, 18-19bm; SuperStock, 12-13, 15, 18-19tm.

Printed in the United States of America at Corporate Graphics in North Mankato, Minnesota.

TABLE OF CONTENTS

CHAPTER 1

THE LARGEST LIVING BIOME

The ocean is the largest **biome** on Earth. It covers 71 percent of the planet's surface.

It holds 97 percent
of all Earth's water.

There are five oceans on Earth. They are all connected in a single body of water. Close to a million types of plants and animals live in the ocean.

WHERE ARE THEY?

The five oceans are the Atlantic, Pacific, Indian, Arctic, and Southern.

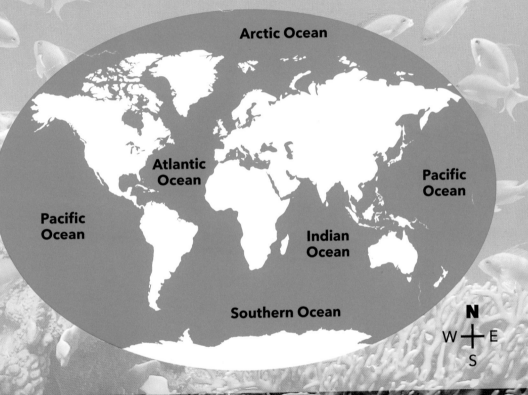

Arctic Ocean

Atlantic Ocean

Pacific Ocean

Pacific Ocean

Indian Ocean

Southern Ocean

N
W E
S

CHAPTER 2

THE OCEAN FOOD CHAIN

All living things need energy. Plants get it from the sun. Animals eat plants and other animals.

A **food chain** shows what they eat. An ocean food chain starts with plants and ends with **bacteria**. Each link in the chain is a living thing. And each gets its energy from the one before it.

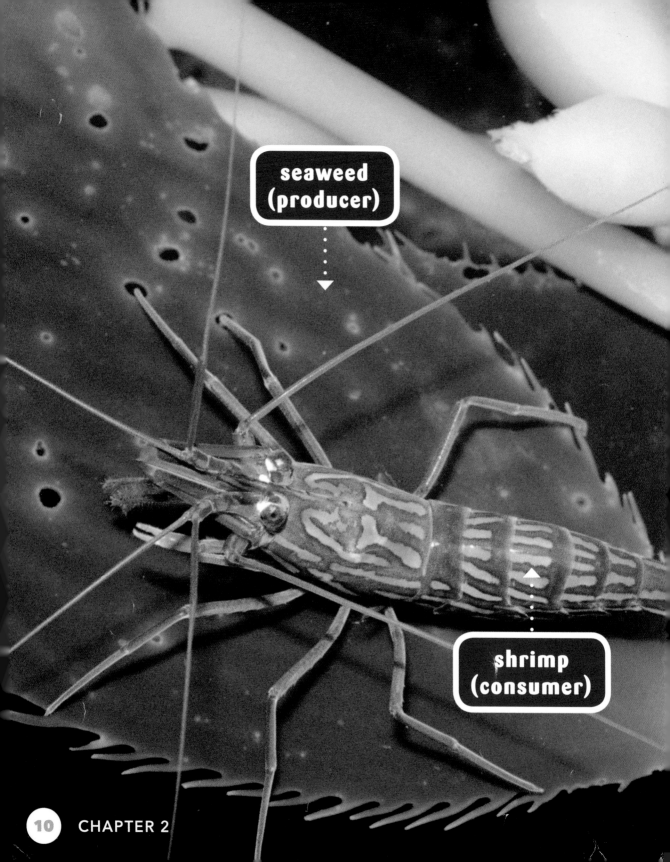

seaweed
(producer)

shrimp
(consumer)

Plant plankton and seaweed are **producers**. They are the first link in the ocean food chain. These plants use the sun's energy to make their own food.

Shrimp, **animal plankton**, and other small creatures eat these plants. They are the second link. They are **consumers**.

DID YOU KNOW?

There is seaweed in some brands of ice cream! It makes ice cream thick.

Fish, seals, and whales are the next link in the chain. They are **predators**. They eat consumers and other predators.

Sharks are a top predator. They eat other predators such as larger fish and seals. Who else are top predators? We are! People eat a lot of fish.

seal
(predator)

shark
(top predator)

CHAPTER 3

FOOD CHAIN CLOSE-UPS

Let's look at a simple food chain.

Plant plankton grows in the ocean.
A clam eats the plankton.
A starfish eats
the clam.

A stingray eats the starfish. In time, the stingray dies. What happens next?

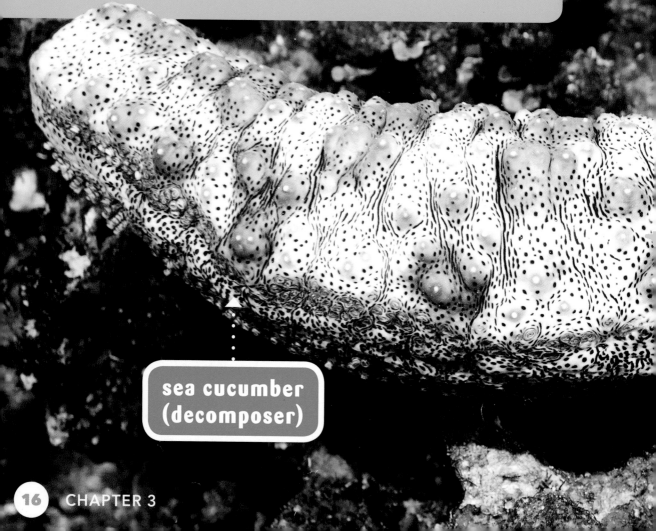

When an animal like the stingray dies, **decomposers** such as bacteria break down the bodies. They change the dead matter into **nutrients**. The nutrients then return to the ocean.

Sea cucumbers help, too. They eat bits of dead matter on the ocean floor.

sea cucumber
(decomposer)

TAKE A LOOK!

One ocean food chain might look something like this:

Producer:
Sea Grass

Predator:
Seal

Decomposer:
Bacteria

Consumer:
Fish

Top Predator:
Shark

Let's look at another food chain.

1) Seaweed grows in the ocean. It gets its energy from the sun.

2) A sea urchin eats the seaweed.

3) A sea otter eats the sea urchin.

4) A killer whale eats the sea otter.

When the killer whale dies, bacteria break down its body. Nutrients return to the ocean.

The food chain starts again.

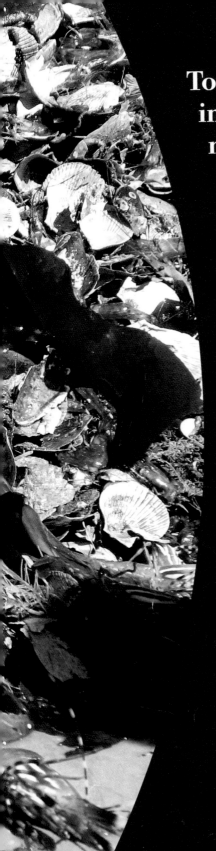

Today ocean food chains are in danger. **Pollution** is killing many of the animals that live there. People are **overfishing**. It is up to us to keep the ocean and its many food chains healthy.

ACTIVITIES & TOOLS

BUILD A FOOD WEB

In this book, you explored several ocean food chains. Can you think of more? Get some paper and a pen. Start at the beginning by drawing a picture of a producer.

What comes next? Think about what might eat that producer. Draw a picture of that consumer, and use a line to connect it with its food. Add links to the food chain by adding predators and finally decomposers.

Now try changing one of the links by drawing a new plant or animal beside the original. Does the next link change? How about the link after that? Keep going, connecting the links with arrows.

Now you have made a food web. A food web shows the way a number of different food chains interact with one another.

GLOSSARY

animal plankton: Tiny ocean animals.

bacteria: Tiny life forms that break down dead animals.

biome: A large area on the earth defined by its weather, land, and the type of plants and animals that live there.

consumers: Animals that eat plants.

decomposers: Life forms that break down dead matter.

food chain: An ordering of plants and animals in which each uses or eats the one before it for energy.

nutrients: Food or other elements that help ocean animals live.

overfishing: Lowering the number and variety of ocean animals by too much fishing.

plant plankton: Tiny ocean plants.

pollution: Harmful or poisonous materials that people add to an environment.

predators: Animals that hunt and eat other animals.

producers: Plants that use the sun's energy to make their own food.

INDEX

TO LEARN MORE

Learning more is as easy as 1, 2, 3.

1) Go to www.factsurfer.com

2) Enter "oceanfoodchains" into the search box.

3) Click the "Surf" to see a list of websites.

With factsurfer, finding more information is just a click away.